3·2·1
MARRIAGE

Participant Guide

3·2·1

Journey from vow

MARRIAGE

to VICTORY

JOHN & JULIE COLLIER

Participant Guide

SEMESTER 1

Birmingham, Alabama

321 Marriage—Participant Guide
Life Bible Study
An imprint of Iron Stream Media
100 Missionary Ridge
Birmingham, AL 35242
IronStreamMedia.com

Library of Congress Control Number: 2023942083

Cover design by twolineSTUDIO.com
ISBN: 978-1-63204-127-2 (paperback)
ISBN: 978-1-63204-128-9 (ebook)
1 2 3 4 5—28 27 26 25 24

CONTENTS

WEEK 1   Introduction 1

WEEK 2   Building a Foundation for Marriage, Part 1 9

WEEK 3   Building a Foundation for Marriage, Part 2 23

WEEK 4   Building a Foundation for Marriage, Part 3 31

WEEK 5   Biblical Foundation: The Husband, Part 1 38

WEEK 6   Biblical Foundation: The Husband, Part 2 45

WEEK 7   The Role of the Christian Wife 49

WEEK 8   Communication: The Number-One Problem
in Marriage 60

WEEK 9   Communication: Marriage, Forgiveness,
and Offense, Part 1 71

WEEK 10   Communication: Marriage, Forgiveness,
and Offense, Part 2 78

WEEK 11   Great Expectations, Part 1 86

WEEK 12   Great Expectations, Part 2 95

ANSWER KEY 103

INTRODUCTION

From the Creators, John and Julie Collier

Welcome to *3-2-1 Marriage*! We are John and Julie Collier, and we are excited to embark on a journey together with you toward a deeper understanding of God's (beautiful) unique design for Christian marriage.

As a couple, we are passionate about marriage, and it is our desire for you to learn how to become one and fulfill the divine beauty God had in mind when He created marriage.

We developed and have been leading this material for many years and have witnessed the miraculous power of doing marriage God's way in so many couples. We cannot wait to share it with you, and our prayer is that as you walk through the small group Bible study, your marriage will be strengthened and realigned and will fulfill the divine purpose God has for you as a couple!

Marriage is a sacred covenant, and a new creation that reflects the very nature of God Himself. In Genesis 2:24, it says, "Therefore a man shall leave his father and his mother and hold fast to his wife, and they shall become one flesh." This spectacular yet profound mystery reveals the depth of God's heart for the intimate union between a husband and a wife: we are to become one! Husband, wife, and Holy Spirit intertwine and transform from three to one (3-2-1)! It is a glorious transformation we are invited to experience as Christ followers!

Our story as a married couple will help you see why we are so passionate about marriage and have given so much of our lives to helping married couples move toward God's design for marriage. We met in college and were married after graduating. It was a wonderful day filled with joy and hope. We expected to live "happily ever after" and were so excited about entering into marriage together.

Early on, our marriage seemed to be going smoothly—we were involved in a local church, served in leadership, were involved in small groups and each having our daily quiet times with the Lord. We did all the things normally expected of a young couple who love Jesus and want to serve the Lord. However, we soon began to realize that something was missing in our marriage.

We were both saved at a young age, raised in Christian homes, and surrounded by Christian community throughout our dating and engagement. But we struggled to walk marriage out God's way and sensed a decline in our unity over time. We eventually got to a point in which we were living in a state of withdrawal from each other. Because we did not have the tools or understanding to become one, we had each caused a lot of pain to the other and did not know how to find our way back to where God wanted us to be as a couple. It was a time that felt very dark in our marriage, and we did not know what to do.

It was in this difficult time that we simply began to cry out to God and ask Him to save us. We began the hard but necessary journey of asking God how to do marriage His way and letting Him knock down the walls and put us back together as He originally designed for our marriage. We slowly started praying together. We started praying over and for each other.

As we laid down our own lives and expectations, we witnessed a true miracle from the Lord, and He began to teach us straight from His Word what He had in mind when He created marriage! Our spiritual lives had been disconnected, but God began to lead us by His Holy Spirit and weave us together into ONE! Holy Spirit, husband, and wife . . . becoming ONE!

Out of our story, the Lord birthed our marriage curriculum. And it has become our joy and passion to share it with others! We have now had so many wonderful years living out marriage as God designed, and we can truly tell you: marriage as God designed is spectacular! It will far surpass what you can hope, dream, or imagine!

Our prayer is that you can have a fresh start and invite God into your marriage in a way you have never experienced—whether you are in the first year of your marriage, still in your early years, or, like us, have been married thirty years or longer. God loves you so much, and He will keep knocking at the door of your marriage until you let Him in, until you lay down all of your "good plans" in exchange for His plans—the *best* plans for your marriage! He has an unbelievable blessing in store for you and your marriage.

As you begin this journey, remember that you are not alone. The Holy Spirit is your guide, and He will give you the courage and strength to move with courage and vulnerability as you share your struggles and victories, the glorious process of becoming ONE.

We are praying over every couple as you learn and understand how to become one as in Genesis 2:24. The journey from vow to victory really means that, from the wedding day until death, you experience the beauty and mystery of becoming one. What a beautiful picture of God's faithfulness and the image of Christ and His church.

Let's begin the journey together. Victory awaits!

Why Marriage?

Read Genesis 2:24.

Have you ever thought about why God created marriage? Marriage was God's idea, after all. That means God gets to define it, and He knows what makes it work.

1. This verse is the _____ of marriage.

This verse tells us that you leave everything and that every other relationship takes a back seat to marriage. That means your parents, your children, every other relationship.

Read Matthew 19:4–6.

What does Jesus say about this verse in the New Testament? Jesus quoted this verse from Genesis and took it even further. Jesus looks back to creation and God's intent in forming man and woman and in establishing marriage.

2. God created marriage for His _____ and our _____.

Read Genesis 2:15–25.

What are ways this entire passage shows us the priority of marriage to God? The first marriage in the garden was the most beautiful wedding setting in history. Sorry, folks, but your wedding may have been in an incredible venue, but it doesn't compare to paradise made by God Himself. The garden of Eden was a paradise with its beautiful surroundings, with the perfect relationship in intimacy Adam had with Eve and both had with God.

3. As beautiful as Eden was, what made it such a paradise was the unhindered _____ that Adam and Eve had with God and with one another.

We live in a consumer-driven world that gives too much focus to surface things like how nice a home is or your beautiful landscaping. Here's the truth: it doesn't matter whether you live in a beautiful garden or in a shack, when you have intimacy with God and with one another, you will be extremely fulfilled. Adam and Eve had that.

Our hearts yearn for that to this day. St. Augustine said a prayer we can all relate to: "You have made us for yourself, and our heart is restless until it finds rest in you."¹ We're made in the image of God, and our hearts are still yearning for that perfect intimacy with God and that intimacy with one another.

If marriage is so important to God, why is marriage sometimes so hard?

Read Genesis 3:1–15.

4. _____ came and brought brokenness into every relationship.

We see, beginning with Adam and Eve, that marriages aren't perfect, and ours will not be. Theologians call this the *fall*. But God who is full of mercy and grace did not leave us in our sin. He lovingly made a way for us to experience new life and a relationship with Him through faith in His Son Jesus.
How can we see the promise of the good news in Jesus in Genesis 3:15?

Although brokenness extends to every relationship, including marriage, Christ also redeemed the marriage covenant. We see the New Testament describe Christ's relationship with the church, Jesus being the groom and the church being the bride.

Let's look at Jesus and His role as husband. He is our role model, men. He is our role model to show us how we're to love our wives. He's our role model for how we live our lives. Jesus loved His bride

---

1 Saint Augustine, *Saint Augustine's Confessions*, trans. Henry Chadwick (New York: Oxford University Press, 2009), 3.

so much He laid down His life for her. Are we loving our bride that same way?

We will have weaknesses; we are self-centered and married to another self-centered person. We all carry baggage into our marriages. We all carry pain into our marriages. We all fall short. We all need mercy. But also remember that marriage is a covenant, which means the person you're married to is the person God wants you to be with.

Our Hope for You in This Study

The Christian marriage should be the most fulfilling, the most successful, and the most honored relationship. It is second only to our personal relationship with God through Jesus Christ. We have Christ as our leader and guide in our marriage. We can look at Him and see how we're supposed to live our lives and how we're supposed to live in our marriage. For us to have the intimacy and joy available to us will require intentionality, faith, and prayer. We won't drift into it; we have to be intentional.

As you walk through this study together as a couple, you will have to make a daily decision to shut the door on the world and what the world is saying about relationships because its advice is broken. Devote yourselves to do it God's way. Yes, it can be more difficult for us to do it His way because of how confused and corrupt the world's view is on relationships today. But you can be sure that God will give us the strength and the power to do it through His Spirit.

Today, as a couple, you can begin a new journey in your marriage with a renewed focus on the Lord and His purposes in marriage.

You will be learning some specific practices to help you to become more like Christ in your marriage. These include praying together daily, a weekly conversation we call a "Starbucks moment," and learning to communicate so that when you have conflict—and you will—you can move from withdrawal to intimacy.

Without including your name, write down a brief answer to each of these questions.

1. What do you hope to learn personally from this study?
2. What is a specific area where you want to see growth in your marriage?
3. How ready are you to learn, to grow, and to be changed?

BUILDING A FOUNDATION FOR MARRIAGE, PART 1

Matthew 7:24–29

P.L.E.A.S.E.—The Keys to Building a Firm Foundation in Your Marriage

Structures not built on a firm foundation will fail the test of time. Eventually, they will crumble to the ground. That is why you must decide for yourself what foundation you will build your marriage on. Will it be God and His ways, or you and your ways? What beliefs, habits, and expectations do you bring with you as you begin this building process, and how do these affect your marital foundation?

It is crucial that you know and believe wholeheartedly what truly brings life and vitality to your relationship from the very beginning. Once your foundation has been established, you can begin building upon it. However, you must ensure that every brick you lay is in line with the foundation of God's Word. This takes faith, prayer, work, and intentionality. Remember, your wedding ceremony is your starting point, not the finish line. You will need to continually invest prayer, faith, time, effort, knowledge, and emotional energy into your spouse/marriage in order to grow together upon the foundation you are building for your marriage.

Without an intentional pursuit of God and building our marriage on Him, we simply drift downstream with culture and suddenly find we are on an unstable foundation.

GROUP DISCUSSION

Read Matthew 7:24–29.

If we want to build on the Rock, what must we do?

_____

_____

_____

_____

_____

How does this differ from building on sand?

_____

_____

_____

_____

You must decide what will be the foundation of your marriage. It's one of the most important decisions you will make in life and one you will need to return to again and again.

> **Time + Unintentionality = Failure**

GROUP DISCUSSION

Read Romans 12:1–2; Deuteronomy 24:5; and Matthew 19:5.

How do these three passages help in establishing the foundation of your marriage?

_____

_____

_____

_____

_____

How important is it to be intentional as a couple?

_____

_____

_____

_____

_____

Read Galatians 6:7.

Compare/contrast God's way versus cultural norms of our day.

_____

_____

_____

_____

_____

A Gospel Foundation

GROUP DISCUSSION

Read 1 Corinthians 15:1–7.

What does Paul say is of first importance for the believer?

_____

_____

_____

_____

_____

How do we apply that to our marriage?

_____

_____

_____

_____

_____

P.L.E.A.S.E.

The P.L.E.A.S.E. acronym is designed to highlight fundamental elements of biblical marriage. Taking the time to grasp these ideas and intentionally and apply them to your marriage will assist you in laying a firm foundation.

P Is for Prayer

1. _____ **together daily:** Invite God to be in the center/guide in the building blocks of your relationship. There is nothing more important for your marriage than daily prayer together as a couple. If you aren't doing this, start today. Don't worry if it seems awkward or if it hasn't been a practice you share, just get started.

> **From John**
> Be yourself when you pray together. When I pray, it's simple and to the point. When Julie prays, it's beautiful, like a poem, descriptive and lovely; you could write them down and put them in a book. Doesn't matter. God cares about prayer from

the heart. So be yourself. God just wants your heart to invite Him into your marriage.

From Julie

Don't be critical of your husband's prayers. His prayer will look and sound different than yours. That is OK! Don't correct him. Be thankful and know that God is at work in all of our prayers.

2. The most intimate act between a man and a woman is

_____ _____ . Your goal is to develop spiritual intimacy in your marriage (Matthew 7:7–8; Matthew 18:19–20; 1 John 5:14–15).

It is important to know the divorce rate for Christian spouses who pray together is less than 1 percent, while those who do not pray together have a divorce rate of approximately 50 percent.[2] Praying couples are also happier, more satisfied with their marriages, and less prone to conflict.

GROUP DISCUSSION

Read Matthew 7:7–8; Matthew 18:19–20; and 1 John 5:14–15.

How do these verses motivate spouses to pray together?

Practically, how might prayer together look in a marriage?

What hinders couples from praying together?

Discuss how praying together increases spiritual, emotional, and physical intimacy.

---

2 Donald R. Downing, *Marriage from the Heart: A Revolutionary Approach to Covenant Marriage* (Maitland, FL: Xulon, 2010), 75.

Let prayer be a first response and not a last resort. For example:

Example A: Bill and Sally have been praying together since they got married. They try to pray for one another throughout the day, but they also set aside time each day to pray with each other. They aren't perfect spouses, but the more they realize their imperfections, the more they are driven to their knees. As they ask God for help to love one another better, He shows each of them areas in which they are acting selfishly. He then draws them to depend on Him for greater measures of Christ like love, and with each passing day—by God's grace—they are learning to love each other more and more selflessly.

Example B: Jack and Mary, on the other hand, offer up a hurried blessing before each meal, pray a little bit on their own, but never pray together. It's not that they meant to leave that out, they just always figure there will be time to do it later— and later never comes. Over time, they grow continually more irritated with one another over little things, grow bitter, and quietly begin to drift apart. One day, after a huge argument, they realize just how bad things have gotten. They decide to ask God for help to restore their marriage, but with all the wounds they've inflicted on each other, there's little doubt that the road to healing will be a long and painful one.

How do these testimonials encourage you to pray together to build spiritual intimacy?

_____

_____

_____

_____

_____

3. Continue to invest in one another through intentional acts of
_____. It's important that we define love according to God's Word as a building block in your marriage (1 John 4:7–8; Colossians 3:12–15; and 1 Corinthians 13:4–7).

L Is for Love

GROUP DISCUSSION

Read Romans 5:6–8.

How does this explain God's love for us?

_____

_____

_____

_____

_____

God, who is holy and perfect, loves us unconditionally in spite of our imperfections. Is love measured by the character of the one giving or receiving?

_____

_____

_____

_____

4. List at least three things your spouse does that make you feel loved.

_____

_____

_____

Did any spouses share the same answers? Do we have a tendency to love our spouse as we desire to be loved? "Love is not love unless it is received by the one being loved."

Read Ephesians 5:25–29, 33; and 1 Peter 3:1–2.

Discuss how husband and wife are to love each other.

_____

_____

_____

_____

_____

Example: While dating/engaged, Billy and Sally talked very much during dates and through texts, phone calls, and messages. This made Sally feel very loved by Billy, and she couldn't wait until their marriage so she could be with Billy all the time. She envisioned late nights talking and deep conversations every day as when they were dating. Billy loved talking with Sally. She was always so respectful of him and complimented him often. She would cook for him and take him meals when he was working late. After the marriage, he envisioned Sally cooking for him often, and building him up with her words and presence. However, once the wedding was over, Billy came home from work tired and often did not want to talk about his long day. He would often want to watch the game or a movie. Sally, also tired from her day, would not want to cook for Billy but would just want to go out. Billy wondered, *What happened to the happy cook who always built me up?* and Sally wondered, *Where is my once talkative Billy?* How will they make sense of this change in their relationship?

When does love for your spouse become an action/decision versus an emotion?

_____

_____

_____

_____

_____

5. Our love for _____ should motivate us to love/respect our spouses unconditionally (1 John 5:3).

6. God's love for _____ shows us how much He loves us so we can love each other well (Romans 5:8).

When is it most difficult to love our spouses?

_____

_____

_____

_____

_____

Do we have a plan for loving/respecting them when they do not deserve it?

_____

_____

_____

_____

_____

The answer to that question will determine the type of marriage you will have. Do you desire a marriage built on the sand—or the Rock? (Proverbs 3:5–6; Matthew 7:24–29)

7. **Remember: _____ first and ask the Lord to help you. He is faithful even when we aren't.** He gave you the wonderful gift of marriage, and He created you to be an instrument of agape love to your spouse. When you love God, you will love one another. What will be your foundation? (Psalm 127:1; Matthew 7:7–8)

A man full of the Spirit of God will love his wife "as Christ loved the church and gave himself up for her" (Ephesians 5:25). A woman full of the Spirit will respect her husband "as to the Lord" (Ephesians 5:22). As a result, they will both bring one another closer to the Lord through their marriage and point a lost world to Christ (Romans 8:9).

A Practical Aid: The "Starbucks Moment"

By "Starbucks moment," we mean a weekly time you get together as a couple to talk about things that are vital in your marriage. For you it may be a "Chick-fil-A moment," a "let's go for a walk moment," or something else that fits. The key is to have these regular meetings to talk about life and your marriage **and to do so when you are not tired, stressed, or hurt**. If this is not a regular part of your marriage you can start now and include discussing things you are learning in this study.

NOTE: This week each of you will need to take a few minutes and take the "Love Languages" quiz at https://5lovelanguages.com/. This is an excellent way to help establish a baseline for understanding how to love and serve one another more effectively.

Review and Application

1. What kind of marriage do you both desire?

_____

_____

_____

_____

2. What are the building blocks of your marriage going to be?

_____

_____

_____

---

3. Do you both agree to trust God and His way? What does that mean for each of you individually? Do you both have to be intentional?

---

4. Do you both desire to grow in being one spiritually? If so, do you commit to pray together daily? Discuss the importance of unity in marriage, and how to build unity apart from God—is that possible?

---

5. How do you both see love? Does your spouse know? How can you communicate your love language to one another? Do you have to be intentional?

WEEK 2

BUILDING A FOUNDATION FOR MARRIAGE, PART 2

Matthew 7:24–29

P.L.E.A.S.E.—The Keys to Building a God-centered Foundation (*continued*)

Review Matthew 7:24–29. If we want to build on the Rock, what must we do? How does this differ from building on sand? You must decide what will be the foundation of your marriage.

P stands for _____

L stands for _____

> **Remember: Time + Unintentionality = Failure**

Marriage is a gift from God, and we have seen that living out our marriage according to His ways is our gift back to Him. *If you are newlyweds, you are building the foundation of your marriage.* If you have been married for some time, you can strengthen or, if necessary, rebuild your foundation. Wherever you are in your marital journey,

God is for you! Reviewing the foundation of marriage is an ever-vital need.

Whether you realize it or not, your marriage is based on something. Will you live your marriage based on the Word of God or something else? It is very important to learn, begin, and continue habits in your relationship that are consistent with God's word that will bring life, vitality, and intimacy to your marriage. Let's talk about what God's word says about marriage, and what you can do to make sure your marriage is based on the Rock? What is the Rock? (2 Timothy 3:16–17; Romans 12:1–2)

GROUP DISCUSSION

Read Genesis 2:18; 1 Peter 3:7; Malachi 2:13–16.

How do these verses show how your marriage affects your relationship with God?

_____

_____

_____

_____

_____

Has society abandoned a God-centered marriage? What has been the impact of this?

_____

_____

_____

_____

_____

1. The first two building blocks that should be present in a Christian marriage are _____ together and _____ (Genesis 25:21; 1 John 4:19; Ephesians 5:25, 33).

2. Note: love is spelled " _____ " to the husband.

E Is for Evangelize

3. We are commanded to _____ our spouse (Ephesians 5:25–27; 1 Peter 3:1–2).

Our words *gospel* and *evangelism* in the New Testament are actually the same word: *euangelizo*. We see evangelism practiced when believers tell unbelievers the good news so they can receive forgiveness and become followers of Jesus.

There's another way to think of the gospel, or good news, that relates to believers who've received salvation. Salvation is the beginning of a journey made possible by good news, but the same good news also guides us on the journey as we grow throughout our lives.

But even as we have experienced salvation, we still get pulled back to self-righteousness. That's why Paul kept reminding believers in his epistles to keep focused on the gospel. We have to keep evangelizing ourselves or as some put it, we keep preaching the gospel to ourselves.

Christian couples evangelize each other as we remind each other of the truth of the gospel. If Jesus's work on the cross and resurrection can save us for all eternity, He can also help us in the daily issues we face in our marriage, and that's good news!

After reading Ephesians 5:25–27 and 1 Peter 3:1–2, what does *evangelize* mean to you? Do you see your marriage as a mission field opportunity?

_____

_____

_____

_____

_____

How do we live out these verses? (*Hint:* John 14:15–16)

_____

_____

_____

_____

We have a tendency to love only when we feel loved. However, this is not how God loves us. He has called you as His children to take upon His nature to love as He loves. God's love is *agape* love, which in Greek is translated as unconditional and sacrificial. This means the husband loves his wife even when he feels disrespected. This also means the wife respects her husband even when she feels unloved.

When we as a married couple choose to love unconditionally when we feel unloved or disrespected, we bring our spouse to the Lord. God designed the marriage covenant to be a sanctifying relationship when we agree to love God first and most and then love our spouse unconditionally as Ephesians 5:25–27 says.

A Is for Ask

4. We should continue to _____ : "How can I make you feel more loved?" (Matthew 19:5–6; Philippians 2:3–8).

Continue the things you did when you were dating/engaged that made you want to get married in the first place: humility, perseverance, love. Your marriage is not defined by a few big moments but rather in the small day-to-day moments of prayer, love, mercy, grace, and forgiveness given freely to one another consistent with God's word.

Marriage is a life of humility, service, and teamwork. It's the gift you give that keeps on giving—to you! What degree of expertise do you have with your spouse? Do you know what makes them feel love from you? Our love for God and our walk as a follower of Christ has everything to do with our marriage. Love God first, then you are able to love your spouse.

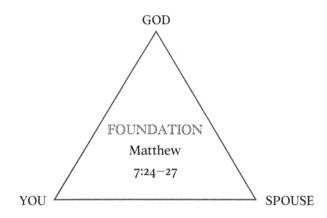

What will be the foundation of your marriage?

Review and Application

Read Romans 12:1–2.

1. What are ways you can apply Romans 12:1–2 to your marriage?

_____

_____

_____

_____

_____

2. As we have discussed so far, the foundation of a godly marriage includes *prayer*, *love*, *evangelize*, and *ask*. After reading Ephesians 5:25–27 and 1 Peter 3:1–2, do you see the God-given power

you possess in the life of your spouse? Are you acting as a light pointing your spouse to the Lord?

_____

_____

_____

_____

_____

3. Knowing the unconditional love of the husband leads his wife to holiness, should the husband be motivated to love his wife?

_____

_____

_____

_____

_____

4. Knowing the unconditional respect of the wife leads her husband to the Lord, should she be motivated to respect him?

_____

_____

_____

_____

_____

5. How has praying together the past couple of weeks changed your relationship?

_____

_____

_____

_____

_____

Through the unconditional love of the husband and unconditional respect of the wife in the Christian marriage, the marriage is "God centered" and points a lost world to Christ Himself.

Husbands—pray and ask the Lord to help you love your wife unconditionally. Have a plan for loving her when she does not deserve it.

Wives—pray and ask the Lord to help you respect your husband unconditionally. Have a plan for respecting him when he does not deserve it.

Together, discuss what you both agree will be the foundation of your marriage—The Word of God (the Rock) or something else (the sand). Ask God to help you, and He will!

You are building the foundation of your marriage on something whether you are intentional or not. As you learn the biblical foundation of marriage, you will have to "live it out" intentionally.

BUILDING A FOUNDATION FOR MARRIAGE, PART 3

Matthew 7:24–29

Will you build your marriage on the Rock? (Matthew 7:24–27)

God gave us His Word to bless us and show us how to live. But He also gives us the freedom to accept or reject His Word. This verse discusses the difference between those who hear and obey, in contrast with those who only hear. It is a blessing to know that if we follow His Word, He is faithful to hold us, protect us, and bless us as His children.

Thank you, Lord! Our love for our heavenly Father is measured through obedience (2 Timothy 3:16–17; John 14:21, 23; Ephesians 5:15–17).

In Ephesians 5:16, Paul tells us to make the best use of our time. The New Testament has two words for time. One is *chronos* and means time like on a calendar or our watch, and the other means time as in the significance of the time, as in an important season. That word, kairos, is what Paul uses here. As we review our lives, we can see seasons of life: some are like spring, full of promise and joy; some may be like winter, harsher and more difficult. Marriages have seasons: the honeymoon, early years of marriage, the season of having children, the season of grandparenting, and more. As a couple, you want to be aware of the challenges and joys of the season you are in, and as Paul said, make the most of each season.

REVIEW

P _____ with and for one another daily (Matthew 18:19–20). Rate of divorce less than 1 percent.

L _____ your spouse as he or she desires to be loved with God's love (1 John 4:19–21; Ephesians 5:33).

E _____ one another (1 Peter 3:1–2; Ephesians 5:25–27).

A _____ how can I love you more (Philippians 2:2–4)?

S Is for Study

1. Invest in your relationship with God through the daily _____ of God's Word. The more intimate your relationship with Christ, the more your life and marriage will bear the fruits of the Spirit. His commands are not burdensome to us when we are filled with His Spirit. Daily fellowship and prayer are the foundation of your marriage! (1 John 5:3; Mark 1:35; Galatians 5:16, 22; John 7:38)

How do we not conform to the world but instead be transformed? (Review of Romans 12:1–2)

Your marriage will not look exactly as you dreamt it would. Your spouse will not always meet your expectations. You will see their weakness more often than you would like.

However, if you allow, God can take those unrealized expectations and make something beautiful! He wants to bless you both with abundant life (John 10:10)—a life that is beyond your wildest dreams. But remember, He has a desire for us to be holy, and that often requires a degree of discomfort. If you allow Him, He will use your marriage as a method of sanctification to transform you, to bring you closer to what He desires you to be. This might be painful at times but will result in holiness in your life that you would likely never be able to attain otherwise.

Based on the paragraph above, how can Matthew 16:24–25; Luke 22:42; and Proverbs 3:5–6 apply to your marriage?

_____

_____

_____

_____

_____

2. You need to continue to have a habit of _____
your spouse.

What is important to them? What makes them feel your love? What are their favorite foods and activities? Continue dating after marriage and remember that there will be many seasons of learning and growth.

GROUP DISCUSSION

Read Philippians 2:2–4. List the statements describing how to treat one another.

_____

_____

_____

_____

_____

How is it possible for you to live this passage out in your marriage?

_____

_____

_____

_____

_____

E Is for Example

3. Finally, your marriage should be an _____ to a lost world and point them to Christ. He created marriage to bless you, give you intimacy, to raise godly children, and to further His kingdom and purpose. Decide whether your marriage will draw others to Christ (including your children), or if it will draw others away from Him. Decide what you want the foundation of your marriage to be. You get to decide—rock or sand?

Read James 1:22. Discuss how this verse shows that how you "live out" your marriage determines your witness to a lost world.

Review and Application

Review what the foundation of your marriage will be, including these key ideas:

P—Pray together; this is critical to your marriage.

1. Have you begun praying daily together? If so, what have you learned so far? If you are still working toward this, what might the main issues be that hinder you from praying together?

_____

_____

_____

_____

_____

L—Love one another unconditionally, as God loves us.

2. Do you think daily first of loving your spouse or of your own needs? How might you show love to one another this week?

_____

_____

_____

_____

_____

E—Evangelize one another, reminding each other of the good news.

3. What are ways the gospel can help you to encourage one another this week? Ideas: Jesus forgave us far more than we will ever have to forgive; we received amazing grace from God; we have been redeemed for a purpose; because we know God, we have the power to serve Him personally and in our marriage through the Spirit; etc.

_____

_____

_____

_____

A—Ask each other how you can help your spouse feel more loved.

4. What are some simple ways you can ask one another about this?

_____

_____

_____

_____

S—**Study God's Word** and one another.

5. Can you share something you learned from God's Word this week with your spouse that's helped you to know and serve the Lord more effectively?

_____

_____

_____

_____

_____

E—**Example:** Be an example to the world through your marriage.

6. How can you pray and ask God to help you to be a godly example in your marriage?

_____

_____

_____

_____

_____

BIBLICAL FOUNDATION:
THE HUSBAND, PART 1

Ephesians 5:25–30

Compare and contrast how the world views the role of the husband in family and society versus the biblical view.

Where do we find the TRUTH of the role of the man in marriage? (2 Timothy 3:16–17; Romans 12:2; and Hebrews 4:12)

The primary responsibility of the husband in the Christian home is to lead as God's Word instructs us. Husbands, you are to love your wife, not as the world loves, but as Christ loves the church and gave Himself for her. This is a sacrificial, self-denying kind of love. Your role as head or leader of your home does not give you the right to dominate and control but to lead like Jesus. To do that, we must be surrendered to Jesus ourselves.

1. The husband must FIRST _____ to Christ and experience God's unconditional love in His own life (Luke 10:27).

2. The husband must be _____. He is to know and understand his role. The primary ambition in his life is to love God, and to love his wife unconditionally. He understands **the Holy Spirit is the source of his love, strength, wisdom, and guidance**. If he relies on the culture or his male instincts to direct him, he will fail miserably. He understands the authority and responsibility given to him by God to serve, lead, and sacrifice for his wife and family.

He (1) rejects passivity, (2) leads courageously, and (3) accepts responsibility. He does NOT conform to this culture and worldview as we saw in Romans 12:2.

Time + Unintentionality = Failure

3. The husband is to _____ **his wife as Christ loved the church and gave himself for her** (Ephesians 5:25).

He loves by:

A. Unconditional _____ (Ephesians 5:25–27). Do you love unconditionally?

What are ways you've been taught or shown how to love your wife in the past? How do those compare to how Jesus loves His bride?

B. Learning what makes her _____ (Deuteronomy 24:5). What are things you know that make her happy? Is this something you need to learn more from her?

C. Leaving and _____ (Genesis 2:24). Do you know how to be "one" with your wife?

D. Protecting _____ (Mark 3:27; 1 John 4:18). Do you know what makes her feel safe?

E. _____ **and cherishing** (Ephesians 5:28–29). Do you know what your wife needs?

Read John 14:15; 14:21; 1 John 5:3. It is of utmost importance to love God first and most—to love Him and obey Him. If you don't love your wife, it is usually because you have stopped loving God.

How can these verses help motivate the Christian husband?

_____

_____

_____

_____

_____

John's Story

In our thirty years of marriage, we've seen this. At one point my pride had us far apart emotionally, but over the course of several years we saw that gap closing, so that after five years we were much closer. That's the beauty of marriage because the more you become one, the more you become known and love together, the more you'll see so many beautiful things come out of your marriage and so many discoveries of different seasons of life. The energy that fulfills all that, everything that makes that run, is your spiritual connection. We learned this from the simple, daily practice of praying together. When we were in the depths of our marriage, when our marriage was really bad for the first ten plus years, Julie really didn't want to pray with me sometimes even after we started praying together. There was a breakdown of trust. Sometimes I would just hold her on the shoulder and pray over her. But over time, as the days and weeks passed, she really warmed up to it so much. And now we're at a point where we won't go a day without praying together. I'd be afraid to, to be honest.

If he loves God, he will love his _____ as Christ loves the church. How did Christ love the church? He gave Himself for her (sacrificial love, Ephesians 5:25). If he does not love God, he will _____ love his wife unconditionally. *His priorities and motivation will be from God, not man or what he feels.*

4. He is the _____ of his wife as "Christ is head of the church." This is an *unconditional* statement whether he realizes it or not. He is the head of his family (1 Corinthians 11:3; Ephesians 5:23). Headship is translated in Greek as *kephale* and often means the physical head of the body, the cornerstone of a building, or an authority figure. *Kephale* can also mean the "source" as in the source of a spring.[3] Headship means that everything that flows into the marriage/family will come through the husband. This means that he is responsible for his marriage for his family. If there is any

---

3 John R. Markley, "Head of the Church," ed. John D. Barry et al., *The Lexham Bible Dictionary* (Bellingham, WA: Lexham Press, 2016).

dysfunction in his marriage and family, it is almost always traced back to the man and his role as husband and father. God will hold the husband accountable for his marriage and his family. Just as Jesus was called to love, give, and sacrifice for the church as head, so the husband is called to love, give, and sacrifice for his marriage as Christ did as the head in His marriage.

Take-Home Discussion for the Husband

Husband, it is your role in headship to build a safe place where you and your wife can have deep, intimate conversation without fear of punishment and where you are both secure enough to speak without taking things personally. These questions reflect the lesson and offer a place to discuss these during the week.

Ask your wife:

1. What do I do that makes you feel love?

_____

_____

_____

_____

_____

2. What do I do that makes you happy?

_____

_____

_____

_____

_____

3. What do I do that makes you feel "oneness" with me?

_____

_____

_____

_____

4. What do I do that makes you feel safe?

_____

_____

_____

_____

5. What is one fruit of the spirit that you would like to pray for me?

_____

_____

_____

_____

These questions are a good starting point to have a positive discussion on how to be the husband God called you to be. Try not to be discouraged or overwhelmed by this discussion. Knowledge is power. How can you know if she never shares with you? Remember, you are on the same team. She is for you! When you love one another, you are actually loving yourself. You are "one flesh."

WEEK 6

BIBLICAL FOUNDATION:
THE HUSBAND, PART 2

Ephesians 5:25–30

Husbands, what were some helpful things you learned from your take-home discussion?

_____

_____

_____

_____

_____

What does headship mean for the husband according to the New Testament?

_____

_____

_____

_____

_____

How does that compare with culture today?

_____

_____

_____

_____

_____

Examples of headship in marriage: Genesis 3:6; Philippians 2:7–8; Romans 5:19.

We can see the contrast in Romans 5:19 between two husbands and their legacies. Adam (the first "one man" listed) brought the legacy of sin, but Jesus (the second) brings a legacy of righteousness. A husband or father who does not exercise headship in a kind, gentle, selfless manner slanders God and jeopardizes not only his own eternity but also those who are closest to him.

C. S. Lewis said, "This headship, then, is most fully embodied not in the husband we should all wish to be but in him whose marriage is most like a crucifixion; whose wife receives most and gives least, is most unworthy of him, is—in her own mere nature—least lovable. For the Church has no beauty but what the Bride-groom gives her; he does not find, but makes her, lovely."[4]

1. The husband is _____ for his marriage and family.
He will be held accountable for the salvation and direction of his

---

4 C. S. Lewis, *The Four Loves: The Much Beloved Exploration of the Nature of Love* (Orlando: Harcourt, 1960), 105.

marriage/family. As the man goes, so goes his family. When a man follows God and submits to God's leadership, his family follows after him (Ephesians 6:4; Colossians 3:2).

2. He is to be the _____ **of his children** (Ephesians 6:4; Colossians 3:21).

> Statistics from fatherless homes: 5 times more likely to commit suicide, 9 times more likely to drop out of high school, 20 times more likely to end up in jail. [5]

Discuss the spiritual impact of men fulfilling or not fulfilling God's role in Christian marriage and in society.

3. The way he treats his wife affects his _____ **with God** (1 Peter 3:7; Malachi 2:13–15).

4. Even Christlike husbands will _____ (Psalm 37:23–24; Proverbs 24:16; Isaiah 41:10). We will stumble and that's okay. We want to keep learning and growing. Jesus is the only one who never sinned!

5. It is a _____ **walk.** Your level of spiritual maturity and ministry will never exceed your role as husband (Matthew 6:33; John 15:7; Philippians 3:13–14). What will your legacy be as a husband?

---

5 "Research and Statistics," Rochester Area Fatherhood Network, http://www.rochesterareafatherhoodnetwork.org/statistics.

Just as we discussed, God made male and female very different, so expect a time of learning and adjustment. But remember, YOU are responsible for your marriage and family.

A Reminder of God's Kind of Love

Love is _____ and _____; love does not _____ or boast; it is not _____ or rude. It does not _____ on its own way; it is not irritable or _____; it does not rejoice at _____, but rejoices with the _____. Love _____ all things, _____ all things, hopes all things, _____ all things. (1 Corinthians 13:4–7)

"*Love* is to put yourself in the place of another, to feel their feelings, walk in their shoes, weep with their tears, rejoice in their joys, take upon yourself their burdens, and give to them your life. . . . When you feel it and when you don't, it doesn't matter—it doesn't change anything. . . . We can only receive it and be changed by it. We can only let it change us."[6]

---

6 Jonathan Cahn, *The Book of Mysteries* (Lake Mary, FL: Frontline, 2018), day 12

THE ROLE OF THE
CHRISTIAN WIFE

Ephesians 5:22–24

Compare and contrast how the world views the role of the wife in family and society versus the biblical view. Where do we find the TRUTH of the role of the woman in marriage (Ephesians 5:33; Genesis 2:18)?

The primary responsibility of the wife in the Christian home is to respect and submit to her husband. She was created to be her husband's helpmate. She intercedes for her husband through prayer, submission, and respect through the power of the Holy Spirit in her life. God designed her role to be one of strength, which is of utmost importance in her life and the life of her husband.

1. You were created in the image of God to be an _____ to your husband (Genesis 1:27; Genesis 2:18).

As wives, we are to be a helper, or *ezer kenegdo*, for our husbands. *Ezer kenegdo* is translated in Hebrew as "lifesaver." The same Hebrew word in scripture used here for the woman is used elsewhere in the Bible only to refer to God the Father, God the Son, and God the Holy Spirit! It is a phrase of honor and significance, not an assignment to a lesser person or a second-class individual. God chose to use the same word for woman that He uses when describing God himself coming through for mankind . . . when it is desperately needed and is a matter of life or death!

What an exciting call on the life of a woman!

What are some ways we can "save" the lives of our husbands?

_____

_____

_____

_____

_____

When you begin your marriage, you can hardly wait to set off on a new adventure—husband and wife ready to face life's ups and downs together. Similar to two people in a hot air balloon, you are excited to take off and begin your journey. You see your spouse through rose-colored glasses and are convinced you have married the Ferrari of all men. Surely all of your dreams will come true and many more!

ezer kenegdo ("life saver")
- Respect him.
- Speak words of life and encouragement.
- Pray for him.
- "Speak" his love language (physical affection).
- Thank him for all he does.

However, it does not take long to realize that our spouses are far from perfect (and we are too)! If you envision your marriage as a hot air balloon soaring high in the sky, you might be concerned when you begin to realize this hot air balloon has holes of imperfection. We begin to notice the flaws in our husband: angry outbursts, the messy floor, or a lack of attention to our needs. Slowly we see how what we thought was a Ferrari appears to be more of a Pinto!

He never helps at home.

He leaves clothes on the floor.

He has flaws (e.g., angry outbursts)

As wives, our first instinct is to see the "holes of imperfection" in our hot air balloon and point them out to our husbands. Minor irritations become large frustrations, and as we repeatedly share our thoughts on our husband's shortcomings, the small holes in the hot air balloon become larger. Over time, the hot air balloon does not seem to be flying so well, and we are not sure what has happened—all we did was point out the areas that "needed to be fixed"! Why does the entire balloon seem like it is about to crash?!

Have FAITH and BELIEVE
that God is working miracles
in your husband and in
your marriage.

When you build up your husband—**feed the "fire" of the Spirit**—
the hot air balloon takes off and you BOTH soar together.

Without the help of God's Word, we as wives think it is our job to point out the flaws and shortcomings in our husbands. And when he doesn't change, we think we need to speak louder, more frequently, and perhaps add in some eye-rolling or a slammed door.

We are then utterly frustrated when these antics do not make our lives better. Instead, we feel more distant from our husbands.

It is time to call for help! God's ways are so much better and higher than our ways! God wants us to pray over our husbands, believe the best about them, speak life over them, and have faith even when we can't see the outcome.

Here is our opportunity to be a lifesaver for our husbands, to see their potential, and to pray over their failures and weaknesses (the holes in the balloon). God wants us to act in faith, believe our husbands are in the process of becoming mighty men of God, and watch Him work miracles! We must use our words not to tear down but to call out the impossible in our marriages as we pray and intercede for our husbands. When we do this, we notice the fire that causes the hot air balloon to fly gets stronger and the hot air balloon begins soaring higher and stronger! As we agree with what God says about our husbands, despite what we see, we get to witness the transformation God has for them and it becomes a blessing and a miracle—and God uses US, the wives, the lifesavers, to take part in this amazing miracle!

Another beautiful part of this picture of the hot air balloon is that as we build up our husbands and our marriage, we realize it is a blessing to us as well! We are both in the hot air balloon together, and as it soars, as we bless and pray for our husbands, we truly thrive in a soaring marriage as God intended!

Faith: God is able. God will. We allow the Holy Spirit to call out the impossible in or marriage as we pray and intercede for our husbands. As we agree with what God says about our husbands, despite what we see, we get to witness the transformation God has for them, and it becomes a blessing and a miracle we take part in and benefit from.

2. You are to, above all else, _____ and be _____ to your husband (Ephesians 5:22–24, 33; Colossians 3:18; and Titus 2:5).

After the fall of Adam and Eve, God told Eve, "Your desire will be for your husband, and he shall rule over you" (Genesis 3:16b). God was saying that she would have a sinful and selfish desire to control Adam, to usurp the man's headship, and Adam would have a sinful desire to dominate and control Eve. How do we escape these sinful desires in our marriage, and live out the role God Himself has for us as His followers? The Christian wife must submit to Christ! (Ephesians 5:22)

"Submissive" is the Greek word *hupotasso*, which means to get under and lift up or to put in order. It's a military term, as in when a soldier lines up in formation under a commanding officer. It is not a demeaning term that minimizes the soldier; it is a term that recognizes both roles as they relate to others in the military formation.

What does it look like to respect your husband? Does your love for God lead you in your role as wife?

As stated with the husband, though the husband and wife are equal in their standing before God, in order for the family to function in harmony, the woman, with no loss of dignity, takes the place of submission to the headship of her husband.

Discuss 1 Corinthians 11:3. Does this mean Christ is inferior to God?

When the woman seeks to usurp this authority and rule the home, havoc results and the home is left wide open for spiritual attack (Isaiah 3:12).

Our husbands are a spiritual covering for us, like an umbrella that protects us from the rain. As long as we stay in the place of godly submission, we are protected from needless spiritual attacks the enemy wants to "rain down on us." However, if we choose to usurp our husband's authority and rule the home ourselves, havoc results and we are left open for spiritual attack and so is our home.

Thought: Submission is easier if we as wives feel secure and loved. This is God's plan

3. Your role as wife is _____ (1 Peter 3:1-2)

Does this role of the wife depend on the behavior of the husband?

_____

_____

_____

_____

_____

Julie's Story

When John and I were first married, I truly thought I was a submissive wife. But I came to realize just how easy it is to fall into subtle forms of manipulation and control. I sometimes see things John doesn't see, which can be frustrating. But when that happened, I wasn't always honoring or respectful toward him. And if we are honest, it is easy for us as wives to make our husbands feel like idiots if we are not careful.

I cannot control my husband's decisions and at the same time expect him to be in the role that God called him to be as the leader of the home. I have to focus on my role as a wife and trust the Lord to work in my husband's life. It is my role to pray for him, respect him, and watch God move! The incredible thing is that as we continue to grow on this journey, I have seen God do miracles and real transformation.

Staying focused on God and His purposes will bring us to an evangelical focus, taking us back to the gospel. And nothing is as transformational as watching the gospel take place in our marriage.

Even when the husband is unsaved or saved and not walking with the Lord, when we as wives choose to align with God's plan of submission, the Lord will deal with our husbands in His time and in His way!

Wives are called to submit to the headship of their husband, and husbands are to submit to the headship of Christ and love their wives as Christ loved the church. The issue is not superiority or inferiority. It is about God's order in the home. Most important, it is about obedience to God! (Philippians 2:1–4)

4. Your role is a position of _____ and _____ in God's kingdom (Romans 12:1–2).

Discuss how a wife displays her strength in God's eyes. How does this compare to what the world tells us?

_____

_____

_____

_____

_____

Discuss how our emotions as a wife can be used for good or evil. How does God want us to control our God-given gift of emotions?

_____

_____

_____

_____

_____

5. You have the power to tear down your _____
(Proverbs 14:1; 21:19; 31:18; 31:10). As wives you are made by God to be a source, through the power of the Holy Spirit, of nurturing love in the home, and you are priceless.

What can a wife do to build up or tear down her husband? Are her motives always inherently evil?

_____

_____

_____

_____

6. It is a daily walk born out of a heart and love for
_____ (Psalm 37:4; John 14:15).

Discuss how love for God motivates you to follow His Word. Will your affections follow?

Take-Home Discussion

Discuss with your husband:

1. What you do to make him feel respected, and what you do to make him feel disrespected.

_____

_____

_____

_____

_____

2. How unconditional love and unconditional respect/submission are born out of a love for God. How is it possible for you to perform your role as husband/wife (Ephesians 5:33)?

_____

_____

_____

_____

_____

3. How you both can extend grace/mercy/forgiveness when one stumbles in performing their role. Discuss how communication/openness can help you learn and be intentional (Colossians 3:13).

_____

_____

_____

_____

_____

4. How God's plan for marriage works best when both are walking with God and making intentional efforts in performing their roles to unconditional love/respect (Galatians 5:16).

_____

_____

_____

_____

5. How important is it that you agree to pray together daily and agree to follow God's design for your marriage? Discuss how unity in marriage is only possible when you both agree to do marriage God's way (Matthew 7:24–27).

_____

_____

_____

_____

_____

COMMUNICATION: THE NUMBER ONE PROBLEM IN MARRIAGE

Ephesians 4:29

Communication is said to be the number one problem in marriage. Through Scripture, we know that "death and life are in the power of the tongue" (Proverbs 18:21). In Ephesians 5:4, Paul tells us that there must be "no [none, zero] filthiness" in our speech. This means that when we talk, there is to be purity and love in our speech, and we should especially practice this in our marriage.

Our words have great power, especially in marriage. They should be gentle, ready to yield—not always insisting on your own way or your own viewpoint. Paul writes in Ephesians 4:29, "Let no corrupting talk come out of your mouths, but only such as is good for building up, as fits the occasion, that it may give grace to those who hear." The word translated "corrupting" in this passage actually means "rotting" or "decaying."[7] In Genesis 2:24, we see it is God's desire is for you to be one flesh spiritually, emotionally, and physically with your spouse. This bonding cannot happen without

---

7 Harold W. Hoehner, "Ephesians," in *The Bible Knowledge Commentary: An Exposition of the Scriptures*, ed. J. F. Walvoord and R. B. Zuck, vol. 2 (Wheaton, IL: Victor Books, 1985), 637.

excellent communication skills. These skills have to be continually learned and refined.

Read the following:
- James 3:3–11
- Proverbs 10:19
- Matthew 12:34–36
- James 1:19

What are your main thoughts about communication after reading these?

_____

_____

_____

_____

Discuss how married believers should communicate. Do we sometimes fail to realize the power of the tongue to speak life or death?

_____

_____

_____

_____

_____

There are three states in marriage:

Intimacy—Conflict—Withdrawal

A Christian marriage is a covenant between two followers of Jesus under God's authority, but the two followers of Jesus are still sinners. No matter how much you love one another, there are times you will disagree, argue, and have conflict. Learning to face these times of conflict in prayer to resolve them together will move us from conflict back to intimacy. But when we fail to resolve a conflict, it will lead us to withdraw from one another. One of the most powerful ways to keep growing in your marriage is to learn the simple line above and fight for each other to move conflict to intimacy.

John and Julie's Story

Early in our marriage, we didn't see a lot of conflict in our home. It was there; we just didn't perceive it. But as our marriage continued, we started having more conflict because everybody has conflict. That's part of the reality of relationships.

As newlyweds, when we did notice conflict, we ran from it. We would have an argument; we wouldn't resolve it, and where did we go? To withdrawal, withdrawal that brought pain because we were made to live in intimacy. Intimacy is where you're going to be the most content and happy and feel so much joy and peace because you chose to resolve the conflict and not run from it. As we learned this concept as a couple, it changed our marriage, and it will change yours, too!

How do we transition from a state of conflict to a state of intimacy? Where do you want to live? Discuss the difficulty in remaining in a state of intimacy.

_____

_____

_____

_____

_____

How do we learn to get back to intimacy? Through communication. That's why communication is so important. We have to talk it out in ways that build each other up, not tear each other down. We fight for our marriage and for one another rather than fight against one another.

Suggestions for Excellent Communication

1. _____ **together daily.** Fight your battles on your knees. Give thanks in all circumstances and pray through your struggles. Pray first! (Matthew 15:18–19). Discuss the effect praying together has in your marriage communication.

2. _____ **before you have a difficult conversation** (1 Thessalonians 5:16–18; James 1:26; and Luke 6:45). Have a plan. Use Ephesians 5:25, 33 as a filter for your words to one another.

Discuss how communication in your home growing up affects the way you communicate now. How important it is to agree to the

Lord's standard (Ephesians 4:29)? Unless you are intentional, you will likely do the same.

3. Learn and commit to good communication _____!
Timing is crucial: don't have a difficult discussion when either one of you is tired, stressed, or hurting (Proverbs 12:18; 25:11; and Galatians 5:15). It's not always what you say but how you say it.

Starbucks Moment

4. Do not let Satan get a _____ (Ephesians 4:26–27).

Discuss the importance of having ground rules for communication (Colossians 4:6).

Four toxic traits to avoid. As the leader discusses the following toxic traits with the group, use the space to record your own thoughts about them.

Criticism

_____

_____

_____

_____

_____

Contempt

_____

_____

_____

_____

_____

Defensiveness

_____

_____

_____

_____

Stonewalling

_____

_____

_____

_____

5. Remove the _____ _____ (Genesis 2:25; 3:7). Be completely honest about how you feel about your needs, desires, dreams, and wants. This requires deep emotional transparency. Don't allow any subject in your marriage to be off-limits.

Never assume your spouse knows your needs or expectations. Remember men and women are different. Don't be frustrated or disappointed if your spouse doesn't completely understand your expectations. Subtle hints do not work (especially for guys!) (Proverbs 13:12).

If you do not communicate your feelings, desires, thoughts to one another, do they simply just go away? Do you have to continually learn how to communicate as one? How do you balance Ephesians 4:29 and Genesis 2:25?

_____

_____

_____

_____

_____

6. Women communicate _____ times more than men. Conversation to a woman is like _____ to a man.

Discuss types of communication together. Be proactive and intentional. The goal is proactive, not radioactive communication.

7. Request, inform but do not _____. Only God can change your spouse. Prayer and your actions are powerful, not your words (Proverbs 21:19; 27:15; and 1 Peter 3:1–2).

Discuss the difference between deep communication and nagging.

8. Toxic communication can be a _____ **problem** (Luke 6:45; Psalm 19:14; and Romans 8:6). Pray for/with one another.

Discuss how to change toxic/unloving/disrespectful communication in marriage.

9. _____ **mercy and grace to one another.** Pursue unity in your communication (1 Corinthians 1:10; Colossians 3:13–14).

Discuss the gift of learning, growing, discovering unity and love in your communication. Agree to persevere together to strive for intimacy and not give up. You will be tempted to settle for withdrawal in exchange for temporary peace (Galatians 6:9).

Your willingness to grow together in your communication will set you up for success as you enter and progress through marriage. Be patient with one another and be willing to forgive.

Resist the urge to place a wall around yourself when hurt. Be completely honest with one another when hurting after a careless word. Trust the Lord and allow Him to direct you in your marriage. His refining in marriage is for your good and the good of your spouse. Pray over your communication together. Love God and love one another in word and deed.

Review and Application

1. Discuss how you observed your parents communicate. Loud? Silent? Sarcasm?

_____

_____

_____

_____

_____

2. How do you want to communicate in your family? You are building a foundation now.

_____

_____

_____

_____

_____

3. Discuss how you can have more proactive discussion and less reactive and radioactive discussions.

_____

_____

_____

_____

_____

4. Is there a radioactive topic in your marriage? How do you change that?

_____

_____

_____

_____

_____

5. Do you have a regular "Starbucks moment"? Intentionality?

_____

_____

_____

_____

_____

6. What tendencies do you have in your communication when conflict arises?

_____

_____

_____

_____

7. Discuss the importance of excellent communication to stay in a marital state of intimacy.

_____

_____

_____

_____

_____

8. Discuss how you two will move from a state of conflict/
withdrawal to a state of intimacy.

_____

_____

_____

_____

_____

COMMUNICATION: MARRIAGE, FORGIVENESS, AND OFFENSE, PART 1

Colossians 3:12–14; 1 Corinthians 13:1; Proverbs 19:11

One of the true blessings in the life of a married believer is the opportunity to be one with the man or woman of your dreams. You will have many moments to love and enjoy the blessing God has given you in your spouse. Through the years, God desires you to enjoy the fruit in the wonderful journey of becoming one. This is truly a blessing, but it will only be possible for those who learn how to forgive and not take offense for the hurt and pain that is inevitable in the marriage covenant. Your spouse will make mistakes, disappoint you, hurt you, and let you down. God will give you the opportunity in your marriage to love as He loves, forgive as He forgives, and live in freedom if you obey Him and have faith in His way and Word. It is your choice—to live as the world lives or to live the life God has created you to experience, to live out the gospel of Jesus Christ.

This is especially true of the marriage covenant. Will you choose to forgive and love as Christ or pick and choose what commands you will follow? Your answer will impact the future of your life and marriage.

We live in a culture today marked by being offended and easily triggered. List some examples of this:

_____

_____

_____

_____

_____

Discuss again the three states of marriage.

Intimacy——Conflict——Withdrawal

Read Genesis 2:24–25; Matthew 19:5; and Ephesians 5:31.

1. God _____ you to be one—to be known and loved completely and unconditionally.

Discuss the fruit of your marriage when you are united as one and in a state of relational intimacy. Have you experienced God's perfect plan of oneness in your marriage? Describe how it feels. Have you experienced withdrawal? How does that feel? It is impossible to live as one if you do not forgive.

2. An offense is unforgiveness that will result in separation, pain, and _____ if not handled correctly.

Offense is more than just being angry, hurt, and disappointed. You can't be in a relationship with anyone in a meaningful way without at times experiencing these. Offense is *holding onto* the hurt, *nursing* bitterness, and allowing the wrong to *harden* your heart and contaminate your emotions and thinking. An offense is allowing pride and unforgiveness to reign in your life. The word *offense* is the Greek word *skandalon*, which is the trigger of a hunter's trap that holds the bait. Taking up an offense is dangerous because it makes the person who is offended blind to the other person's positive qualities and focus on their negative traits. You make a mental list of all the ways he or she has hurt or disappointed you. And, if you are offended enough, it will cause you to vilify them in every way.

Offense will also cause you to accentuate your good traits and focus on how you deserve better. It will also blind you to your own sin, which is pride. Offense creates division, lack of trust, and self-imposed isolation. This isolation only leads to more pain and distortion of truth. You eventually end up far away from God and other relationships. You build up walls and keep people at an emotional distance so you will never be hurt again.

Read Colossians 3:12–14.

As followers of Jesus, we all want to honor Him. But we still sin in this life and fail the Lord and others. We need His help to display the marks noted in these verses. How do we handle hurt so that we can forgive, move back to intimacy, and not take offense?

_____

_____

_____

_____

_____

3. _____ **and go immediately to God in prayer** (Colossians 3:12–14). Remember most offenses are not intentional, but the hurt is real and must be addressed in a productive, loving way. Apply Romans 12:1–2; 2 Corinthians 10:5; and 1 Corinthians 13:1.

A 1999 study of 124 newlywed couples by researchers John Gottmann and Sybil Carrère with the University of Washington found that how each spouse shared and responded to conflict in the first three minutes is a strong indicator in whether or not the couple will divorce.[8]

For instance, 80 percent of the time the wife initiates the issue and does so in the form of a general criticism that impugns the husband's character rather than emphasizing the specific issue. The husband then responds defensively. Of the seventeen couples who later divorced, they all began with much greater displays of negative emotion and fewer positive words. Stable couples gave more positive comments, and husbands did not initially respond with defensiveness. Starting with prayer and asking God to help can calm you both and seek a positive resolution.

Why does an offense from your spouse hurt more than from others? Love requires sacrifice and vulnerability.

_____

_____

_____

---

8 Ellie Lisitsa, "Predicting Divorce from the First 3 Minutes of Conflict Discussion," The Gottman Institute, https://www.gottman.com/blog/the-research-predicting-divorce-among-newlyweds-from-the-first-three-minutes-of-a-marital-conflict-discussion/.

How do you go to God when you have encountered an offense?

How do forgiveness and resolution lead you back to oneness? Discuss the three states of marriage.

What will happen in your marriage if you don't forgive?

How do you know if you have taken an offense?

_____

_____

_____

_____

_____

Read:

- Luke 17:4–5
- Matthew 5:3–5, 7–9, 23–24, 44–48
- Matthew 7:3–5

How do these verses help us see the importance of forgiveness and not allowing unforgiveness to build up over time?

_____

_____

_____

_____

_____

Review and Application

1. As a couple, can you identify areas that more easily create conflict in your marriage (it could be a habit, an attitude, an action, or failing to do something your spouse considers important)?

_____

_____

_____

_____

_____

2. How can developing the marks seen in Colossians 3:12–14 help you as a couple to fight for each other and for intimacy rather than moving toward withdrawal?

_____

_____

_____

_____

3. Why do you think it is easier for us to want grace shown to us than to extend it to someone else? How can you work on extending mercy and grace to your spouse?

_____

_____

_____

_____

_____

COMMUNICATION: MARRIAGE, FORGIVENESS, AND OFFENSE, PART 2

Colossians 3:12–14; 1 Corinthians 13:1; Proverbs 19:11

Remember the three states of marriage:

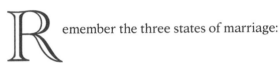

Intimacy——Conflict——Withdrawal

Read again Colossians 3:12–14.

How do we handle hurt so that we can forgive, move back to intimacy, and not take offense?

Last week we learned the first response:

1. _____ **and go immediately to God in prayer.**

Here are more responses:

2. _____ **your heart and mouth** (Proverbs 4:23; 18:21; Psalm 51:10; Matthew 12:34).

Story from John and Julie

> **John:** Recently, we were in the car and were having a good time. It was just the two of us on a beautiful day. The top was

down; the air felt great. It was one of those glorious days. And Julie said, "You know, you don't reach out and hold my hand anymore." I was thinking about how I was really enjoying the drive and suddenly she brought that up. I could have replied, "What are you talking about? You just spoiled a really good drive." But on this occasion, I heeded this point and guarded my heart and mouth. What did I do? I reached over and took her hand.

Julie: Yes, he did!

John: I realized that I love holding her hand. So, instead of being defensive, I reached for her hand, and I've been doing it more since then.

Julie: And I noticed.

The beautiful part about communication issues is when you can say, "Hey, you never reach for my hand," and instead of being met with defensiveness, your spouse responds lovingly.

GROUP DISCUSSION

What does it mean to guard your heart above all else?

_____

_____

_____

_____

_____

How do you guard your heart against unforgiveness?

_____

_____

_____

_____

_____

How difficult is it to guard your mouth when you're hurt? (*Hint:* go to God first.)

_____

_____

_____

_____

_____

3. _____ your feelings with your spouse after you have gone to God in prayer (Genesis 2:24–25; Proverbs 13:12).

How do you communicate your hurt to your spouse in a loving way?

_____

_____

_____

_____

How does going to God first help in sharing your hurt to your spouse?

_____

_____

_____

_____

_____

4. When your spouse is hurt from your actions, _____ and be _____ (Proverbs 15:31–33; 17:9; Ephesians 4:1–5; James 1:1).

Should you ask for forgiveness even when you do not understand how your actions caused pain? Why?

_____

_____

_____

_____

Is this a time for defensiveness and exaggeration?

_____

_____

_____

_____

Is James 5:16 an obvious part of your marriage?

_____

_____

_____

_____

_____

5. _____ **leads to freedom, oneness, and blessing** (Colossians 3:13; Ephesians 4:32; Matthew 6:14–15; 18:21–22; Mark 11:25).

Does forgiveness mean approval?

_____

_____

_____

_____

Does forgiveness always feel good?

_____

_____

_____

_____

What do you feel like when you're forgiven?

_____

_____

_____

_____

_____

Compare and contrast the life of forgiveness and freedom versus unforgiveness and offense.

_____

_____

_____

_____

_____

6. _____ together that God will help you both learn how to forgive completely and to never take up an offense (2 Corinthians 10:5; James 1:25).

Take some time this week to reflect on Jesus, the cross, and how He showed such incredible forgiveness to us. Thank Him for that!

7. _____ the Lord for His example of forgiveness and how to live a life of oneness and freedom (1 Thessalonians 5:16–18; 2 Corinthians 3:17; Luke 23:34; 1 John 1:7).

The Christian marriage should model Christ and His bride, the church. This institution God created should display the gospel to the lost world on how to live and love as Christ. He taught and displayed how to love unconditionally, forgive completely, and live in freedom. The world and its ways will always cry and long for revenge, personal rights, and conditional love. The world cries out, "You will have to earn it, and the person will decide when and how to live, forgive, and love." This, in essence, is creating your own god for your interests. This will result in disunity, separation, and a self-created prison. In every relational failure among believers, one or both parties at some point choose not to forgive, leading to separation, disunity, and offense.

You as a married man/woman will have a decision to make: to live as Christ or settle for what the world offers (Galatians 2:20).

Review and Application

1. Discuss the results of unforgiveness and taking up an offense. Acknowledge the danger of offense.

_____

_____

_____

_____

_____

2. Discuss and share anything you need to ask your spouse for forgiveness.

_____

_____

_____

_____

_____

3. Pray together and ask the Lord to reveal any offense you have taken against your spouse or anyone else. Confess and forgive.

_____

_____

_____

_____

_____

4. Extend mercy and grace to one another and discuss how you want your marriage to forgive and to never take an offense.

_____

_____

_____

_____

_____

GREAT EXPECTATIONS, PART 1

Romans 8:28

We all have expectations of life and its direction. This is especially true of marriage. There are so many unanswered questions/expectations that wait to be discovered. This continual process is one of the true joys of life. Questions like: "How happy will we be; what kind of house and neighborhood will we live in; how many children will we have; how will we celebrate holidays; how much money will we have; I'm sure I'll stay home when our children are born; how successful will my career be (or my husband's); I'm sure my husband will always want to talk to me; we will always feel in love; I'm sure we will always want to have sex as much as I desire," and on and on and on. In fact, we all have expectations (maybe subconscious, unknown) about life and marriage. It's based on gender, upbringing, culture, etc. However, should we focus our expectations in marriage on something other than our wants/desires and happiness? Our expectations should be based in the word of God: His will and design for my life versus my will and design, His kingdom versus my kingdom. Have you surrendered your marriage to God? What do we do about unrealized expectations in our marriage? What are your expectations? Do you know? (Jeremiah 29:11; 1 Thessalonians 5:16–18; Proverbs 3:5; Hebrews 11:1)

Misplaced Expectations

Discuss unrealized, unspoken, subconscious expectations (Jeremiah 2:13).

See if you can identify with any of these when you think about the beginning of your marriage together:

1. I will always be _____ with my spouse, and I will always feel _____.

2. My spouse will make me _____. (Don't put your spouse where God belongs!)

3. Everything bad in our relationship will go away when we get _____, but everything good in our relationship will get better when we get married!

4. Husband: my wife will do things just like my _____. Wife: my husband will do things just like my _____.

5. We will never _____ or disagree.

6. My spouse will never _____ me, and I will never hurt my spouse.

7. I will always understand my _____.

8. As long as we love God and each other, marriage will always be _____.

Discuss the potential danger/result of misplaced expectations apart from God. What are ways the world and its expectations of life/marriage affect you in your marriage? How do we overcome this?

_____

_____

_____

_____

_____

Divine Expectations: Isaiah 55:1–2

1. **You should expect God to honor your** _____
together daily to walk in the Spirit and develop spiritual unity in marriage (Matthew 18:20; 1 Thessalonians 5:16–18).

How does unity in marriage reflect your relationship with God?

_____

_____

_____

_____

_____

2. **You should expect to work to have** _____ **with one another with God's help** (Genesis 2:18; 2:24).

How is it possible to live in a state of intimacy in your marriage?

_____

_____

_____

_____

_____

3. Husbands should expect to practice tenderness and unconditional _____ toward their wives, and wives should expect to practice unconditional _____ toward their husbands (Ephesians 5:25; Deuteronomy 24:5; Ephesians 5:33; 1 Peter 3:7).

How is possible for the husband to love as Christ loves? How is it possible for the wife to respect unconditionally?

_____

_____

_____

_____

_____

4. You should expect to strive to _____ and cleave (Genesis 2:24).

How is it possible to leave all and cleave together?

_____

_____

_____

_____

5. You should expect to be totally _____ **with your spouse** (Colossians 3:9).

What is the result of partial or incomplete truth in marriage?

_____

_____

_____

_____

_____

6. You should expect to protect purity in your _____
_____**, remembering that your body is not yours**
_____ (Hebrews 13:4; Proverbs 4:23; 1 Corinthians 7:3–5; Genesis 1:28a).

How is it possible to maintain purity and physical intimacy in your marriage?

_____

_____

_____

_____

_____

7. The husband and wife should expect to know their
_____ (1 Corinthians 11:3; Ephesians 5:25, 33).

How will you know your role as husband or wife?

_____

_____

_____

_____

_____

8. You will be _____ (Exodus 20:14; Matthew 5:28).

How is it possible to be faithful?

_____

_____

_____

_____

Discuss the peace and unity in marriage when your expectations together as a married couple are in alignment with God. How difficult is it to surrender your will and expectations to God?

_____

_____

_____

_____

Discuss how an agreement to follow God and His will in your life and marriage leads to unprecedented unity in your marriage.

_____

_____

_____

_____

_____

We, as believers, should expect to pursue unconditional love, support, and acceptance independently (Philippians 2:4).

Conclusion: My marriage will not be as I expect, and my response to that will determine my life and my relationship with God and my spouse. Try to focus on what you can give, not what you get. Homework: write down as many expectations as you can and share with your spouse openly.

Review and Application

1. What is your ideal picture of a husband? Wife?

_____

_____

_____

_____

_____

2. What is your plan when you don't get what you're expecting?

_____

_____

_____

_____

_____

3. Discuss how you will deal with unspoken, unrealized expectations.

_____

_____

_____

_____

4. What are some expectations you have regarding birthdays, anniversaries, Christmas, and other holidays?

_____

_____

_____

_____

_____

5. What are your expectations on how you will spend weekends, evenings, free time, and so on?

_____

_____

_____

_____

_____

6. Discuss your expectations regarding money: saving, spending, tithing.

_____

_____

_____

_____

7. Discuss how deep, open, honest communication helps with your expectations.

_____

_____

_____

_____

_____

GREAT EXPECTATIONS, PART 2

Jeremiah 29:11

J eremiah tells us that God has a perfect plan to provide and to bless us. However, during unexpected times in life, we are often tempted to wonder, "God, what are you doing here? This does not look like I thought it would." Your marriage is no different.

At every wedding, a man marries the woman he believes will be his ideal wife, and a woman marries the man she thinks will be her ideal husband. Then, as the pages of the calendar turn, they realize their spouse and marriage are not what they expected, and the result is disappointment. What actually happened, however, is they discovered the real person they married, and whether they realize it or not, that is a gift from God. This unsettling discovery can actually be good for a marriage if you learn how to unpack the discovery. Just as you surrendered your life to follow Christ, you will have to learn to surrender your spouse and marriage to God.

What are your thoughts on the above paragraph? Is it wrong to have high expectations?

_____

_____

_____

_____

_____

What are some common expectations for the wife? Husband? Where do these expectations come from? Do you think the differences in expectations will be cause for discouragement/ conflict?

_____

_____

_____

_____

_____

What is an unspoken expectation? What is an unrealized expectation? Why does an unrealized expectation result in so much disappointment?

_____

_____

_____

_____

_____

What is the difference between an expectation, a goal, and a desire?

_____

_____

_____

_____

_____

How do you effectively handle expectations in your marriage?

1. _____ **God with your spouse and marriage**
(Proverbs 3:5; 16:9; Romans 8:28; Ezekiel 36:26–27).

Are you willing to surrender your expectations of your marriage and spouse to God and give thanks?

2. **Pray together that** _____ **will help you both communicate your expectations to one another in an open, honest, loving way.** Proactive communication: Matthew 7:7–8; Proverbs 13:12; Ephesians 4:29.

Pray and seek God, asking, "Do I trust God with my spouse and my marriage, even when it looks different than I thought it would?" Do you let unfulfilled expectations change the way you treat one another?

_____

_____

_____

_____

_____

3. Do not live by what you _____**.** Do not assume your spouse doesn't love/respect you when expectations are not met. Proverbs 3:5–6.

4. Have a plan for effectively facing different _____**.** Examples: "I thought we would save the bonus check" versus "I thought we would take a nice vacation with the bonus check," or "I thought we would go out Friday night with our friends" versus "I thought we would have a quiet dinner at home and watch TV," or "I thought we would get the garage in order on Saturday" versus "I thought we would go play tennis on Saturday."

How do these differences affect your marriage? How does what we learned about communication apply here? Proactive communication? Be intentional and strive for unity and compromise.

_____

_____

_____

_____

_____

5. Speak _____ **over your spouse and marriage when you are discouraged** (Hebrews 11:1).

Discuss the importance of your thoughts/declarations when discouragement sets in.

6. Decide _____ **how you will react when you realize your marriage (spouse) will not meet all of your expectations.**

Who can meet all of our needs (Philippians 4:19; Matthew 6:33; Isaiah 55:8)**?**

Discuss the importance of claiming/understanding/believing God meets all of our expectations/needs/desires and that our spouse is a gift from Him.

7. Take time to reflect as a couple on the spiritual _____ you have seen God provide up till now in your marriage.

Developing the practice of naming and remembering spiritual markers is a way to celebrate victories in your marriage.

Conclusion

Marriage is a blessing from the Lord to you. However, you WILL experience the unexpected with your spouse and marriage. How you handle the loss of your (dreams) expectations will determine the intimacy of your marriage and how you live out your faith. You probably will not have the exact marriage you always dreamt you would have, but if you surrender it to God, it will be an incredible blessing from the Lord above! (Jeremiah 29:11)

Review and Application

1. How will you respond when your spouse or marriage does not meet your expectations? Do you commit to one another that you will discuss and talk through your expectations?

_____

_____

---

2. What are the three most important desires and expectations you have for your spouse and marriage?

---

3. What are some individual goals you have for yourself in your marriage?

---

4. In faith, do you surrender your spouse and marriage to the Lord—even when it looks different than you expected?

---

5. Discuss your ideal birthday, Christmas, anniversary, and other special occasions. Are those descriptions the same as your spouse? How are they different?

_____

_____

_____

_____

_____

6. Agree to be proactive in your communication of expectations.

_____

_____

_____

_____

ANSWER KEY FOR EACH WEEK

WEEK 1
1. Definition
2. Glory, good
3. Intimacy
4. Sin

WEEK 2
1. Pray
2. Praying together
3. Love
4. [Answers will vary]
5. God
6. Us
7. Pray

WEEK 3
P Prayer
L Love
1. Prayer, love
2. Respect
3. Evangelize
4. Ask

WEEK 4
P Pray
L Love
E Evangelize/encourage

A Ask

1. Study
2. Studying
3. Example

WEEK 5

1. Submit
2. Intentional
3. Love
   a. Love
   b. Happy
   c. Cleaving
   d. Her
   e. Loving

If he loves God, he will love his __wife__. If he does not love God, he will __not__ love his wife unconditionally.

4. Head

WEEK 6

1. Responsible
2. Teacher
3. Relationship
4. Stumble
5. Daily

Love is <u>patient</u> and <u>kind</u>; love does not <u>envy</u> or boast; it is not <u>arrogant</u> or rude. It does not <u>insist</u> on its own way; it is not irritable or <u>resentful</u>; it does not rejoice at <u>wrongdoing,</u> but rejoices with the <u>truth</u>. Love <u>bears</u> all things, <u>believes</u> all things, hopes all things, <u>endures</u> all things.

WEEK 7
1. Ezer kenegdo
2. Respect, submissive
3. Evangelistic
4. Strength, honor
5. House
6. God

WEEK 8
1. Pray
2. Pray
3. Skills
4. Foothold
5. Fig leaf
6. Three, sex
7. Nag
8. Heart
9. Extend

WEEK 9
1. Created
2. Isolation
3. Stop

WEEK 10
1. Stop
2. Guard
3. Share
4. Listen, humble
5. Forgiveness
6. Pray
7. Thank

WEEK 11

Misplaced Expectations

1. Happy, loved
2. Whole
3. Married
4. Mother, father
5. Argue
6. Hurt
7. Spouse
8. Easy

Divine Expectations

1. Prayer
2. Intimacy
3. Love, respect
4. Leave
5. Honest
6. Physical intimacy, alone
7. Role
8. Faithful

WEEK 12

1. Trust
2. God
3. Feel
4. Expectations
5. Life
6. Now
7. Markers